Momentous Materials
Rubber

by Dalton Rains

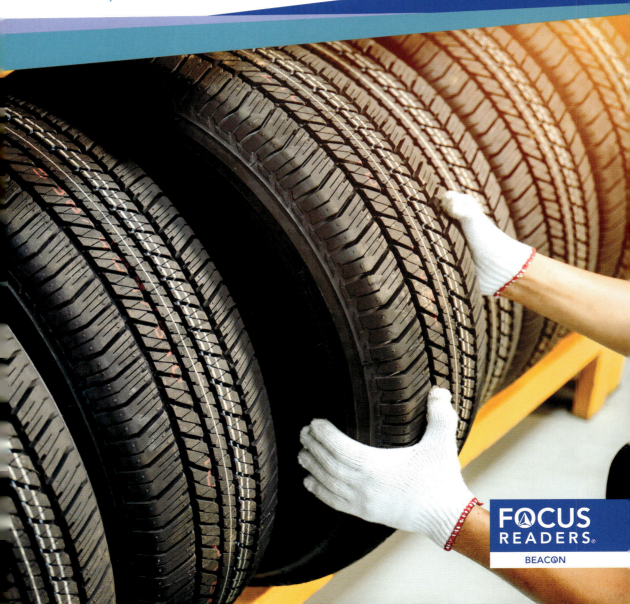

www.focusreaders.com

Copyright © 2024 by Focus Readers®, Mendota Heights, MN 55120. All rights reserved. No part of this book may be reproduced or utilized in any form or by any means without written permission from the publisher.

Focus Readers is distributed by North Star Editions:
sales@northstareditions.com | 888-417-0195

Produced for Focus Readers by Red Line Editorial.

Photographs ©: Shutterstock Images, cover, 1, 4, 7, 8, 11, 13, 14–15, 16, 19, 21, 22, 24, 26, 29

Library of Congress Cataloging-in-Publication Data
Names: Rains, Dalton, author.
Title: Rubber / by Dalton Rains.
Description: Mendota Heights, MN : Focus Readers, [2024] | Series: Momentous materials | Includes bibliographical references and index. | Audience: Grades 2-3
Identifiers: LCCN 2023031238 (print) | LCCN 2023031239 (ebook) | ISBN 9798889980353 (hardcover) | ISBN 9798889980780 (paperback) | ISBN 9798889981602 (ebook pdf) | ISBN 9798889981213 (hosted ebook)
Subjects: LCSH: Rubber--Juvenile literature.
Classification: LCC TS1890 .R325 2024 (print) | LCC TS1890 (ebook) | DDC 620.1/94--dc23/eng/20230711
LC record available at https://lccn.loc.gov/2023031238
LC ebook record available at https://lccn.loc.gov/2023031239

Printed in the United States of America
Mankato, MN
012024

About the Author

Dalton Rains is a writer and editor from Saint Paul, Minnesota.

Table of Contents

CHAPTER 1
Rubber All Around 5

CHAPTER 2
History of Rubber 9

THAT'S AMAZING!
Recycling Rubber 14

CHAPTER 3
Modern Methods 17

CHAPTER 4
Uses of Rubber 23

Focus on Rubber • 28
Glossary • 30
To Learn More • 31
Index • 32

Chapter 1

Rubber All Around

A girl gets ready for school. First, she puts on her shoes. The bottom parts of the shoes are made of rubber. Next, the girl runs outside. She hops on her bike and pedals to school. Her bike has rubber tires.

Rubber is used to make tires for many vehicles, including bikes, cars, and trucks.

The tires help her ride over the bumpy street.

  At school, the girl has a difficult math test. She has trouble with one of the problems. So, she erases a few numbers and tries again. The eraser on her pencil is made of rubber.

Did You Know?

People started using rubber erasers in the 1700s. Before that, people erased pencil marks with bread!

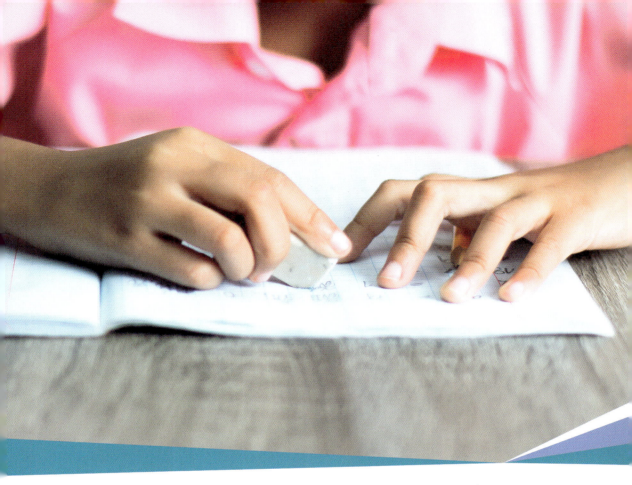

 An eraser lightly scratches the pencil marks off a piece of paper.

After the test, it's time for recess. The girl and her friends play four square. They use a rubber ball for their game. Rubber is all around!

Chapter 2

History of Rubber

Rubber comes from certain kinds of plants. **Indigenous** people in the Americas began using rubber thousands of years ago. In the 1490s, European **colonizers** started taking over the Americas.

 Rubber trees have a white sap underneath the bark. It can be made into rubber.

9

They saw Indigenous people playing games with rubber balls.

In the 1700s, colonizers sent rubber back to Europe. Scientists there learned that rubber was waterproof. So, they used it to make raincoats and boots. However, rubber still had problems. It softened in the heat. It hardened in the cold. It was also sticky.

In the mid-1800s, Charles Goodyear found a solution. He mixed rubber with other materials.

 Rubber boots help keep people's feet dry in the rain and mud.

Then he heated the mixture. This process made rubber more durable. Now, rubber could handle heat and cold. It was also less sticky.

Goodyear called the process vulcanization. His new type of rubber was strong enough to use for tires. Bicycles and cars soon became popular. More and more people needed rubber. So, people set up large rubber farms.

Did You Know?

During World War II (1939–1945), the United States couldn't get enough rubber. So, scientists worked hard to create synthetic rubber.

 By the 2020s, more than 70 percent of rubber was synthetic.

Scientists also started working on synthetic rubber. Progress was slow. But by the 1960s, synthetic rubber was more common than natural rubber.

THAT'S AMAZING!

Recycling Rubber

People often throw away old rubber. Then it sits in landfills. However, dangerous **chemicals** from the rubber get into the ground and air. For this reason, scientists urge people to recycle rubber.

Recycling involves a few steps. First, the old rubber is cleaned. Next, it is broken down into small pieces. Then, the pieces can be used to make new products. Sports fields are one example. They often have rubber in the turf. Even roads can be made of recycled rubber.

A machine breaks old rubber into tiny pieces.

Chapter 3

Modern Methods

Natural and **artificial** rubber are made in different ways. However, some parts of the process are similar. Natural rubber starts in plants. Rubber trees are the most common.

Rubber farmers collect sap in large buckets.

First, workers cut into the tree's bark. That causes sap to drip out. The sap is called latex. Workers collect it in cups. Next, workers add **acid** to the sap. That causes solid pieces of rubber to come together. Those pieces separate from the

Did You Know?

Rubber trees are not the only plants used to make rubber. It can also be made from certain dandelions and fig trees.

 It takes four to six days for a sheet of rubber to dry.

liquid. After that, workers drain the liquid. Finally, they leave the rubber out to dry.

Synthetic rubber is not made from plants. Instead, workers begin with a mixture that includes oil or coal. Then, they combine the mixture with natural gas. This process creates tiny **particles** that can link together. The particles connect to form rubber.

Afterward, both kinds of rubber must be processed. Workers add chemicals. Some of these chemicals strengthen the rubber. Others stretch it. Vulcanizing

 Machines can vulcanize car tires in about 15 minutes.

the mixture makes the rubber harder and stronger. Workers use machines to form the rubber into different shapes.

Chapter 4

Uses of Rubber

More than 70 percent of the world's rubber is used for tires. Rubber is an excellent material for tires. That's because rubber takes a long time to wear down. It can also withstand heat.

More than 300 million tires are sold in the United States every year.

 Rubber belts help car engines work properly.

Rubber is also used in many machines. For instance, belts are made of rubber. Belts help different

24

parts of a machine move. Some machines use rubber hoses, too. Hoses allow liquids and gases to flow easily. Also, rubber gaskets seal the spaces between parts. That helps stop leaks.

Medical products also use rubber. Rubber gloves are one example.

Some people are allergic to rubber. It may cause itching. It can even make breathing difficult.

 Many basketballs are made of rubber. So are the wheels of wheelchairs.

They stop germs from spreading. Rubber tubes can carry blood or other fluids. Rubber straps hold devices onto people's bodies. Some artificial limbs use rubber as well.

Rubber is useful for sports, too. The material can be bouncy. So, many balls are made of rubber. It is also used for hockey pucks. Some types of rubber are soft but hard to damage. That makes rubber a good material for mats.

People use different kinds of rubber every day. This amazing material is an important part of modern life.

FOCUS ON
Rubber

Write your answers on a separate piece of paper.

1. Write a paragraph describing the main ideas of Chapter 2.

2. What is your favorite way to use rubber in your daily life? Why?

3. When did European colonizers first see rubber?
    - A. 1490s
    - B. 1800s
    - C. 1960s

4. What might happen if doctors didn't wear rubber gloves?
    - A. More people would use artificial limbs.
    - B. More people would get sick.
    - C. More people would be healthy.

5. What does **durable** mean in this book?

*This process made rubber more **durable**. Now, rubber could handle heat and cold.*

    A. difficult to find
    B. soft or squishy to touch
    C. able to last a long time

6. What does **turf** mean in this book?

*Sports fields are one example. They often have rubber in the **turf**.*

    A. ground that people stand on
    B. games that people play
    C. balls that people throw

Answer key on page 32.

29

Glossary

acid
A strong chemical that can break down things placed in it.

artificial
Made by humans instead of happening naturally.

chemicals
Specific kinds of matter. Some chemicals can be harmful, and some can be helpful.

colonizers
People who move into an area and take control, often using violence.

Indigenous
Native to a region, or belonging to ancestors who lived in a region before colonists arrived.

particles
Tiny pieces of matter.

synthetic
Made by humans, usually to replace a natural product.

To Learn More

BOOKS

Huddleston, Emma. *Prosthetics*. Mendota Heights, MN: Focus Readers, 2020.

Pearson, Yvonne. *How Do We Classify Materials?* North Mankato, MN: Capstone Publishing, 2022.

Rebman, Nick. *Reduce, Reuse, Recycle*. Mendota Heights, MN: Focus Readers, 2022.

NOTE TO EDUCATORS

Visit **www.focusreaders.com** to find lesson plans, activities, links, and other resources related to this title.

Index

A
Americas, 9

B
balls, 7, 10, 27
boots, 10

C
chemicals, 14, 20
coal, 20

E
erasers, 6

G
Goodyear, Charles, 10–12

I
Indigenous people, 9–10

L
latex, 18

N
natural gas, 20
natural rubber, 13, 17–19

O
oil, 20

P
plants, 9, 17–18

R
recycling, 14

S
sap, 18
synthetic rubber, 12–13, 20

T
tires, 5–6, 12, 23

V
vulcanization, 12, 20

Answer Key: **1.** Answers will vary; **2.** Answers will vary; **3.** A; **4.** B; **5.** C; **6.** A